Customer Service 20: A Team Building Card Game, By Tyler Hayden

Published by Tyler Hayden,
P.O. Box 1112
Lunenburg, Nova Scotia
Canada
B0J 2C0

Cover: Tyler Hayden
Illustrations & Page Design: Steven Lacey
Distributed Electronically by Kindle Direct Publishing

National Library of Canada Cataloguing in Publication

Hayden, Tyler, 1974–
    Customer Service 20: A Team Building Card Game / Tyler Hayden.

ISBN   978-1-897050-58-3

Business. 2. Education. 3. Games. I. Title.

Discover More Fun @ www.teambuildingactivities.com

Customer Service 20: A Team Building Card Game,
By Tyler Hayden

Warning - Use at Your Own Risk

Improper use of the contents described herein may result in serious injury or loss. The activities should not be attempted without the supervision of a trained and properly qualified leader.

FIND THIS FOR **FREE** ... WANT TO GIVE US A HIGH FIVE TO SAY THANK YOU?
We'd love you to BUY US A COFFEE or four - we like coffee.
www.teambuildingactivities.com/store/p46/donate

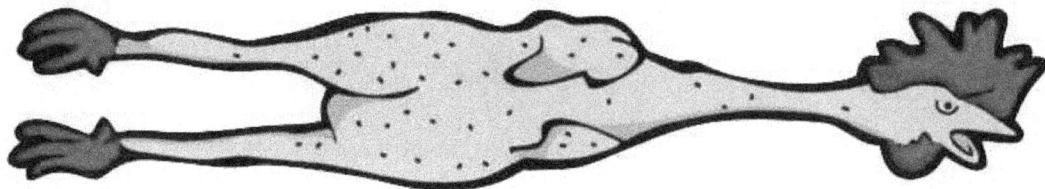

20 Series Games, By Tyler Hayden

This game takes about 10 to 25 minutes to play. It is an incredible content specific icebreaker/break-time activity that is totally inclusive. The educational intention is to encourage people to know a little more about each other in a fun and interactive way while learning a specific core content area (i.e. Customer Service, Leadership, etc). Check out our full line of Team 20 card decks at www.teambuildingactivities.com.

Remember, the priorities are to have fun and play safe.

How to play:

1. Make sure that you have a safe space for the participants to share. Schedule this activity at a time when they will be willing and open to talk to one another. I often run this event during a coffee break or to get the "cob webs" out part way through a meeting and focus the learners thoughts about our specific area of learning upcoming in our program. It is also great to pull it out when you are convening with a group you know fairly well, just for fun.

2. Place the game cards in the middle of the table along with a dice (if you don't have a dice download & make one at www.teammover.com/free).

3. The player with the longest commute goes first and rolls the dice. The person to the rollers right will pick up the card and ask the roller the question. If the player rolls a (1) a Who question is asked - (2) What; (3) When; (4) Where; (5) If; and (6) Why.

4. Once the question is read the roller answers the question. The answering is always "challenge by choice" meaning if they are uncomfortable with the question they answer. If not a new question can be drawn or they can pass on their turn.

5. Players around the table are permitted to ask follow-up questions to the person posing the answer as long as they relate to the original question asked.

6. Play continues sequentially in a clock wise direction.

7. There are two ways to "organize the play" – *Speed Version:* collectively the group answers the twenty questions total - keep track with a tally. *Longer Version:* each person answers a question from each category - keep track with a grid. Either way you need someone at the table keeping track of the "score".

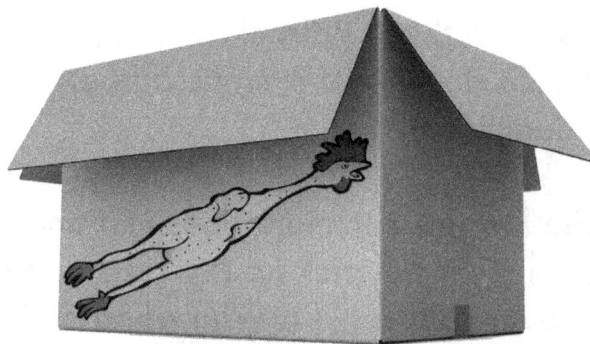

8. Have fun.

WHO 1	is to benefit by engaging in a heated discussion with a customer?
WHAT 2	do you do when a customer complains?
WHEN 3	have you encountered inefficiency in the way we deal with our customers?
WHERE 4	does your job as a caretaker of the customer begin and end?
HOW 5	you are calling back a customer about an issue, what should you know prior to dialing?
WHY 6	is making excuses a bad CRM policy?

© Tyler Hayden

WHO **1**	needs to find out about CRM inefficiencies?
WHAT **2**	is the best way to win over a customer?
WHEN **3**	you are on the phone with a customer, how can you win them over?
WHERE **4**	should you refer a problem you can't seem to solve to the customer's?
HOW **5**	a customer is confrontational, rude, or accusatory, what can you do?
WHY **6**	is doing a satisfaction survey an important part of CRM?

WHO **1**	se responsibility is it to ensure that the customer is pleased with their service?
WHAT **2**	is the difference between listening and hearing your customer?
WHEN **3**	is it important to evaluate the CRM experience?
WHERE **4**	have you experienced excellent customer service?
HOW **5**	you could make one adjustment to improve company wide CRM, what would it be?
WHY **6**	is it important to first understand the "?" from your customer?

© Tyler Hayden

WHO 1	sets the tone for conversations with customers?
WHAT 2	are your three core values when it comes to CRM?
WHEN 3	you are conducting good phone etiquette, what things are you doing?
WHERE 4	can you receive guidance on how we do CRM in our organization?
HOW 5	you could learn one thing that would help you become better at CRM, what is it?
WHY 6	does CRM drive customer loyalty to the organization?

© Tyler Hayden

WHO 1	can you approach to learn new techniques for great customer service?
WHAT 2	do you do that is great CRM?
WHEN 3	you are conducting good face-to-face CRM, what things are you doing?
WHERE 4	have you wished you were videoed because you gave such fantastic customer service?
HOW 5	you owned a store, what would every employee do to ensure great CRM?
WHY 6	are SLAs an important part of good CRM?

© Tyler Hayden

WHO **1**	has given you a great piece of advice for CRM? What was it?
WHAT **2**	are some of the best things you can do to engage a customer in a positive way?
WHEN **3**	is it important to see the world through your customer's eyes? How do you do that?
WHERE **4**	do some customers share their stories of great or poor CRM?
HOW **5**	you could have a better car or q better car service centre, which do you choose?
WHY **6**	is understanding your customer's needs and wants so important?

© Tyler Hayden

WHO **1**	do you speak to if you have a concern with a CRM policy in your organization?
WHAT **2**	is more important to CRM, handling the customer with care or solving their problem?
WHEN **3**	you look at your credentials, what behaviors make you good at CRM?
WHERE **4**	do we need to sharpen our saw for CRM?
HOW **5**	you could stop one pet peeve in customer service worldwide, what would it be?
WHY **6**	is having up-to-date knowledge about products/services so important?

© Tyler Hayden

WHO **1**	**at this table have you seen give great customer service while at work?**
WHAT **2**	**are the biggest challenges to great CRM?**
WHEN **3**	**you look at your credentials, what skills make you good at customer service?**
WHERE **4**	**are we the best at providing customer service?**
HOW **5**	**a customer is having trouble implementing the solution you gave, what do you do?**
WHY **6**	**does the first fifteen seconds of a customer experience yield fifteen years of loyalty?** © Tyler Hayden

WHO 1	have you seen demonstrate great body language with customers?
WHAT 2	two things could management do to reinforce the importance of CRM?
WHEN 3	you are setting up an action plan for your customer, what do you need to consider?
WHERE 4	do you go when you have a positive or negative interaction with a customer?
HOW 5	you could sum up your approach to CRM in one word, what would that word be?
WHY 6	is how a customer feels so important?

© Tyler Hayden

WHO 1	is better at CRM: a dog or a cat? Why?
WHAT 2	does CRM mean to you?
WHEN 3	have you been surprised by a customer?
WHERE 4	do you see our organization having a customer-responsive culture?
HOW 5	something is about to go really wrong with a client's problem, what should you do?
WHY 6	does CRM need to be a culture in the workplace?

© Tyler Hayden

WHO **1**	should be coaching CRM skills to staff?
WHAT **2**	things do others do for you that you think show good CRM when you are the customer?
WHEN **3**	have you been blindsided by a customer's level of satisfaction?
WHERE **4**	do hiring strategies become an influence over CRM?
HOW **5**	we gave an award for the best CRM in our organization, who would win?
WHY **6**	does CRM make your job easier?

© Tyler Hayden

WHO 1	se personality is better for CRM: Martha Stewart or Donald Trump?
WHAT 2	can you do to improve customer service at an organizational level?
WHEN 3	have you surprised yourself in a customer service interaction?
WHERE 4	should employees be evaluated on their customer service skills?
HOW 5	you could choose just one thing to do more often to give great CS, what would it be?
WHY 6	is an employees freedom to make decisions important?

© Tyler Hayden

WHO **1**	**is a great communicator with customers?**
WHAT **2**	**does a customerresponsive culture look like?**
WHEN **3**	**does CRM influence sales?**
WHERE **4**	**do you need to develop your strengths in CRM?**
HOW **5**	**we get an upset client, what should we do?**
WHY **6**	**are our professional skills so important for customer service?**

© Tyler Hayden

WHO 1	are the clients that make doing customer service worthwhile?
WHAT 2	things can you do that will inspire a customer to come back?
WHEN 3	have you been rewarded for great CRM?
WHERE 4	would you like to learn about CRM because you think they do the best job at it?
HOW 5	someone having a bad day had to be frontline CS personnel, what should they focus on?
WHY 6	do people say you are great at customer service?

© Tyler Hayden

WHO 1	is responsible for communicating the possible solutions?
WHAT 2	things are you able to make a decision on when it relates to?
WHEN 3	is flexibility important in customer service?
WHERE 4	in the world have you travelled and experienced a culture of customer service?
HOW 5	you had one piece of wisdom about CRM to impart to a new staff member, what is it?
WHY 6	do you want to provide great service?

© Tyler Hayden

WHO **1**	has really made your job easier?
WHAT **2**	would you like people to say about your CRM on your performance evaluation?
WHEN **3**	is it OK not to stick to the timeframe you promised your customer?
WHERE **4**	do you find customer service in sport?
HOW **5**	there were a master's level course in CRM, what famous person should teach it?
WHY **6**	is CRM central to our business activities?

© Tyler Hayden

WHO **1**	will keep clients in tough times because of their top-notch service?
WHAT **2**	do you use to measure customer feedback and satisfaction?
WHEN **3**	is it OK not to communicate with a client?
WHERE **4**	is the best customer service at a local restaurant?
HOW **5**	animals ruled the world, what animal would be the best at CRM and why?
WHY **6**	do we care what people say to others about our customer service?

© Tyler Hayden

WHO **1**	in your past is really good with (people) relationships?
WHAT **2**	would you like more training on to improve your customer service?
WHEN **3**	is the time you have made a real difference for a client?
WHERE **4**	is the best place to communicate with clients?
HOW **5**	you have a problem with a product, how do you approach the CS agent?
WHY **6**	are we the best at customer service in our industry?

© Tyler Hayden

WHO **1**	in government is the best at customer service?
WHAT **2**	is the value of being concise in your communications with customers?
WHEN **3**	have you gone that extra mile for a client?
WHERE **4**	do happy customers go?
HOW **5**	you could suggest one way we could improve our CRM, what would you suggest?
WHY **6**	do people want our help?

© Tyler Hayden

WHO **1**	in business is the best at customer service?
WHAT **2**	have you done that is over-the-top for a customer?
WHEN **3**	have you added more value to a customer without adding more paperwork for you?
WHERE **4**	is it appropriate to ask for clarification of a client's issue?
HOW **5**	management decided to reward great customer service, how should they do it?
WHY **6**	do we need to measure regularly our effectiveness in customer service?

© Tyler Hayden

WHO 1	on TV demonstrates behaviours that are conducive to great customer service?
WHAT 2	inspires you to provide great CRM?
WHEN 3	should you be accessible to your clients?
WHERE 4	do we need to tweak our CRM model?
HOW 5	you see a co-worker providing a poor level of service, what would you do?
WHY 6	are we so good at CRM?

© Tyler Hayden

WHO 1	sets the vision for CRM?
WHAT 2	is more important: a new customer or a returning customer?
WHEN 3	have you been over the-top impressed with how a client treated you?
WHERE 4	should we log our ideas to improve our CRM?
HOW 5	we were to clone one trait of CS among our employees, what would it be?
WHY 6	does leadership philosophy affect customer service?

© Tyler Hayden

WHO **1**	**are the best types of customers?**
WHAT **2**	**will you do to be the best at customer service?**
WHEN **3**	**have you felt the support of management in your customer service?**
WHERE **4**	**do we need to add some energy in our customer service to improve our results?**
HOW **5**	**our organization showed that it really supported CRM, what would it be doing?**
WHY **6**	**is it important that CRM is part of the corporate culture?**

© Tyler Hayden

WHO **1**	outside of your industry, should you benchmark your customer service after?
WHAT **2**	is the best part about your job as it relates to customer service?
WHEN **3**	do you feel you provide your best service to clients?
WHERE **4**	have you shopped that a salesperson has earned your trust through quality CRM?
HOW **5**	we asked only one '?' of our clients after our CRM experience, what would that '?" be?
WHY **6**	is simple etiquette often the best policy for customer service?

© Tyler Hayden

WHO 1	is a good role model for customer service provision?
WHAT 2	is your favorite part of engaging with customers?
WHEN 3	is customer service worth it?
WHERE 4	did you learn your best CRM trick or practice?
HOW 5	a storybook character could teach CRM, who would be best to do so?
WHY 6	is CRM defined by our culture?

© Tyler Hayden

A Message for you.

Dear Team Mover,

We are so thankful you chose to share one of our 20 Series Books with your Team. We are passionate about helping connect people in meaningful ways by brining the world books, activities and tools like this - because we think people matter.

As we move forward in publishing this (and other) series of books and games, we need your help to build a community of people with that same authentic desire to create meaningful relationships with the people they work with. We ask you join us and share our work with your friends, colleagues and families.

Here are some of the ways that we can stay connected and you can find more resources (link to the appropriate social media links on the sites):

Team Building - www.teambuildingactivities.com
Keynotes & Consulting - www.tylerhayden.com
Books & Consulting - www.14minutementor.com
Books & Giving - www.messageinabottlebook.com

Look forward to connecting soon. Best of continued success my fellow team mover - the work you are doing matters.

Tyler

www.ingramcontent.com/pod-product-compliance
Lightning Source LLC
Chambersburg PA
CBHW051235200326

41519CB00025B/7387